LOCALS

A collection of prose poems

Books by Claire Bateman

The Bicycle Slow Race
Friction
At the Funeral of the Ether
Clumsy
Leap
Coronology
Coronology (and other poems)
Locals

LOCALS

A collection of prose poems

Claire Bateman

SERVING HOUSE BOOKS

Locals: A Collection of Prose Poems

ISBN: 978-0-9858495-2-8

Cover image: John Kroll, a journalist who lives outside Cleveland, Ohio

Serving House Books logo by Barry Lereng Wilmont

Published by Serving House Books

Copenhagen, Denmark and Florham Park, NJ

www.servinghousebooks.com

First Serving House Books Edition 2012

"For all things are made also of what resists them."

—James Richardson, "How Things Are"

Acknowledgments

Selections from "Locals" (some in earlier versions) have appeared in the following publications:

Crashtest—I

Blackbird—IX, XIV, XV, XVI, XVIII, XIX, XXI, XXII, XXIV, XXV, XXVI, XXVII, XXVIII, XXXIX, XL, XLI, XLII, XLV, XLVI, LXXI, LXI,

Camera Obscura—L, LI, LIII, LIV

Extract(s)—XXXI, LV, LVI

Harper's—XXIII (reprint)

Mississippi Review—II, III, IV, VII, X, XVII, XXIII, XXVI, XXIX, L, LXIV

MUSE—LVII, LX, LXXII

The Weekly Hubris—XXIV and XXIX

The author would like to thank Nin Andrews, Sasha Bishop, Sarah Blackman, Bruce Bond, Sarah Efird, Judy Goldman, Mark Halliday, and Robert Solomon for their support and editorial comments.

I

On the first day of spring in this realm, each of the fourth-grade classes must vote on whether or not to proceed toward adolescence. No one ever attempts to play hooky by faking a sore throat or a cough; since kindergarten, the children have been preparing for this election with clandestine alliances and counter-alliances, much rumor-mongering and selling of information true and tainted, all kinds of extortion, espionage, and blackmail, and too many straw polls to track. No adult is permitted to interfere; every crop of children must decide on their own, though the data is far from conclusive. For instance, one child's mother sings all night long but sniffles tearfully into her apron during the day when she thinks no one is watching, and another's child's oldest brother was mirthful and talkative until he reached puberty, when he became steadfastly taciturn—is he morose, now, disenchanted, or does he guard some stupendous secret? How to determine what to make of grownups?—they are potentially dangerous, yet often bored and boring; perpetually exhausted, yet willfully frenetic; resigned, even apathetic, yet always erupting with apparently arbitrary edicts and injunctions.

Despite this torturous lead-up, however, every class manages to arrive at a majority decision. For elections concerning other issues, teachers generally pass around the traditional wicker basket into which the children toss their stained and crumpled yeas and nays, but on this occasion, federally appointed officials tally the votes. And then the teachers distribute colored caps (red for growing up, yellow for remaining at age nine), so that as soon as the fourth-graders begin to surge through the school's double-doors, each waiting parent can know whether to anticipate the eventual arrival of grandchildren or to vie for guaranteed placement at the Home for the Young. After all, what decent family would leave their beloved future orphan to roam with the packs of perpetual nine-year-olds that are gradually taking over the cities?

*

Of all the realms, only this one can boast a near-perfect level of social harmony. Is its population homogeneous, everyone belonging to a single extended kinship group? Or might there be a more sinister reason for such noteworthy concord—a low dose of euphoria-producing pharmaceuticals in the drinking water, perhaps, or even a brainwashing regimen resulting in some sort of hive-mind?

No, this community is not a whit less diverse than any other, and neither water-doctoring nor brainwashing is implemented.

Instead, when an interaction hints at veering toward antagonism, the Dispatching Center deploys a licensed Misinterpreter for whose benefit the entire argument must be ritually reenacted, word for word, gesture for gesture. Then, without even taking time for deliberation, the Misinterpreter diffuses the hostility by unrecognizably distorting all utterances in just a few appropriate phrases so that everyone may return to the task at hand in a state of cheerful, mutually-agreed-upon delusion.

For doesn't the whole world know that conflicts are rarely incited by failures of communication? Only in this realm, however, does public policy compensate for the fact that most people understand each other only too well.

*

III

In this realm, all adult citizens carry Certitude Assessment Receipts to their accountants during tax season, for no belief is tax-free, though the young are less strictly appraised than the elderly, who have had time to develop a little cognitive self-restraint.

Some citizens spread out their certitudes more or less evenly, rendering a small fee for each; others throw almost everything they have into a single belief. And a few maintain a relatively low level of conviction about nearly everything, keeping their credits in high-interest CDs in case they eventually come across someone or something worthy of a supreme commitment—often this sum is still appreciating in value even as its owner is being laid to rest in the ground. In these circumstances, the wealth is transferred to a public fund for assisting people who are so exceptionally and irrevocably dogmatic that they have to declare bankruptcy by the time they are middle-aged.

*

IV

In this realm, though it is with utmost ease that citizens find themselves channeling the ever-vociferous dead, no one is even mildly interested in their complaints, self-revisions, political diatribes, economic advisories, or predictions. The unborn, too, have much to say, but their queries and demands come out in the untranslatable utterances of the before-world. And here also, if a citizen lets down his guard for even a moment, he'll find himself emitting the urgent communications of a passing cat or dog that has chosen to take advantage of his vocal cords; or humming the eerie, chlorophyll-inflected tonalities of local plant life; or announcing the nearest building's ongoing report of minute seismic fluctuations in a choked, mortary murmur that is impossible to comprehend or ignore.

Thus, in this realm of unlimited frequencies, the true challenge is to consistently channel only oneself. Those who do so are considered heroes and heroines, and everyone envies them even though they tend to die young due to the strain of filtering out all the other voices.

*

V

In this realm, the population is still reeling from the flash bulletin wedged between a commercial for composting mulch and a public service reminder about the annual anti-aging vaccine.

"Where were you when you heard?"

"I was in a sports bar watching the game—we just put down our drinks, and sat there, staring."

"We were at the mall, shopping in electronics, and all of a sudden, we saw it lit up on a hundred different screens at once"—

floating in blackness, THE WORLD, one moment assumedly planar, the next, indisputably round.

Now everyone's relationship to the horizon has been irrevocably altered, along with their understandings of gravity, heaven and hell, somnambulism, flight, transcendence, and periphery.

Now there is no way off! Gone the possibility of a balletic leap from the edge!—in its place (of all things) only digging, only "down" and "in"—and where's the allure in that?

*

Each morning in this realm, the people check to see that once again during sleep, they have been reincarnated, or more accurately, reinstated, as themselves, complete with personal histories, memory gaps, and ingrown toenails. Themselves, not "still" but "again." Old people: themselves! Pregnant women: themselves! Even the infants and the unborn, though they don't realize it: themselves!

Occasionally, someone stays up all night—though this person may feign normalcy, the excruciating courtesy that friends and family exude only intensifies the shame of being yesterday's version.

*

One morning in this realm, all the poets, playwrights, and composers woke to find their notations disintegrating on their desks, just as all the artists beheld their fresh colors melting together and their sculptures-in-progress imploding: the allotted amount of negative space in art had been used up, so nothing new could be created.

The actors and musicians didn't mind. There were already more than enough works to keep them employed, and their audiences were palpably relieved to glimpse (for the very first time!) the possibility of, if not actually "catching up," at least not completely going under as they felt they had been doing their entire adult lives.

No, the only ones who actually suffered were the creators themselves, who now rendered otherwise cheerful citizens gloomy by their very presence even when they weren't complaining about the situation, which was hardly ever the case. The formation of grief groups and psychotherapy SWAT teams did nothing to alleviate their misery.

After some debate, the artists were rounded up, herded onto luxury cruise ships, and sent on tours of the realm's islands in hopes that new vistas might cheer them, but when they returned, they were even more unpleasant than they had been before their departure, and the rest of the populace, having grown used to their absence, was less willing than ever to tolerate them. The only alternatives seemed to be interment or mass execution.

So back to the ships they were sent, but this time, the crews refused to accompany them, and now they must swab the decks themselves and do their own cooking. At designated ports, they are provided with supplies and then sent on their way without being allowed to disembark. It is as though all the human restlessness of the entire realm now repines on these ocean liners, while everyone else gets along quite well without it.

*

VIII

When vacations to the past became available in this realm, citizens in their second and third decades of life rushed to view history's dramas, but those in their more mature years chose instead to visit their own parents' younger selves in hopes of extricating them from their varied and mutating configurations of difficulty. No one knows whether or not such attempts were successful, since none of the adult offspring ever re-appeared in their own chronological locations.

Some pundits speculated that this tinkering with history had (predictably) created alternate time streams in which the travelers elected to remain as, in some sense, the guardian angels of their youthful mothers and fathers from whom they were unable to tear themselves away.

Others posited that the rescuers had altered so many past events and circumstances that they had paradoxically (and no less predictably) erased the occasions of their own conceptions. But despite all the public safety announcements ("BEWARE—CONTACT WITH YOUR PARENTS' CHILDHOODS MAY PROVE FATAL!"), people continued to disappear on rescue missions. That is why you can only rarely find in this realm any citizen older than forty-five or so, a demographic calamity that has come to seem completely commonplace.

*

In this realm, the moment the autumn flu hits, everyone immediately heads for quarantine, for the dreaded Precognition Pandemic is notorious for wreaking havoc.

Ironically, it is the mutations producing the slightest and nearest versions of precognition which create the most turmoil, since the stricken individuals find the immediate future so familiar that they remain ignorant of their condition, and don't try to compensate.

No vehicles are allowed on the roads during flu season; if you are suffering a heart attack or giving birth, you are left to your own devices, for all the ambulances must remain firmly in park lest a driver suddenly fall ill and attempt to navigate the terrain he or she "sees" rather than the one the vehicle is actually traversing. This affliction is so contagious that it affects even the unborn, who find themselves enduring their entrance into the world twice, once as febrile hallucination, and once in reality; always after their actual births, they appear lethargic, having been born jaded by their "near- life" experiences.

*

X

In this realm, it is always mail-time, deliveries overlapping like waves as the missives pour in from every direction. The citizens have no concept of a completed interaction, for there is always another thank-you, apology, question, comment, or qualification. An exchange may merge with a pre-existent correspondence, modulate into a sequence of an entirely different mode, and then dissolve into multiple tangentially-related communications. Most of the items are illustrated—many even illuminated—in countless incandescent hues.

The bulk of the mail, however, is composed of silences represented by blank stationary of varying sizes and textures; for instance, a silence in the form of a square-inch of hair-shirt material might elicit a silence in the form of pure unbleached silk which releases a lemony fragrance as it expands to fill the whole room. These caesuras are no less necessary to the postal flow than are musical rests to a fugue or sonata.

Once a year, everyone gathers for the Burning of the Mail, during which all letters since the previous Burning are consigned to the flames. The silences are saved for the end, when everyone steps back and pulls the children close, for it is the unspeakings that burn the brightest, sending out dangerous sparks. And because the only tenet of this realm's religion is that reality itself is an epistolary arrangement, the correspondences begin the next morning exactly where they had been left off, with not even the most insignificant article misplaced.

*

In this realm, no one knows ahead of time when the Coincidence Consultant will arrive, so it's always a surprise when she shows up in her little booth in the town square. Word gets around so quickly, however, that before long, everyone is standing in line to speak with her. Though eavesdropping is entirely against protocol, no one refrains—who, after all, could resist? That's why people tend to whisper when it's their turns, though the Consultant seems incapable of speaking in anything softer than a resonant boom; thus, while the actual coincidences remain more or less confidential, the whole town hears her pronouncements. "The event in question, despite the intricacy of its correlations and the extraordinary nature of its timing, was nevertheless completely random, and conveys no meaning whatsoever; you are quite free to put it out of your mind," she says to one inquirer. "Yes," she says to another, "on a significance scale from one to ten, this occurrence is practically pushing eleven, no question about it," though she leaves interpretation entirely up to the individual—the fact and degree, not the consequences, of an event's meaningfulness are all she conveys. Nobody has ever reported wishing they hadn't spoken with her, though many regret having wasted their opportunity on what turned out to be a worthless coincidence, for she interprets only one per individual, and who knows when—or whether—she might return?

*

XII

Up until not too long ago, every citizen of this realm was frequently accosted and advised by various versions of that individual's future self; despite the fact that these visitors possessed the same genetic material and early memories as the "target" self, they eventually came to be viewed as predators.

For instance, even if a version virtually indistinguishable from that-day's-you had approached you, claiming to be from twenty-four hours later, offering you apparently pertinent business advice, you would have had to summon up all your street-smarts—though you knew yourself to be at that moment as honest as you'd ever been, who knows what odd mental turns the you-of-tomorrow might have taken in those intervening hours, giving in to temptations which that-day's-you couldn't even imagine!   Equally dangerous was the ethically-over-evolved-yet-compellingly-radiant-you urging the current-you to donate a kidney to someone you'd never met, or propose marriage to the next leper you found languishing on a corner.

No less menacing than these extreme selves, however, and much more common, were the ones who wanted to spare you a difficult romance, or merely tell you where to find your missing keys—if heeded, this type of chrono-visitor would leave you spiritless, enfeebled, deprived of the emotional muscle-tone developed only through full engagement with the rigors of uncertainty.   In fact, there was soon such an overabundance of stunted citizens incapable of making real-time choices on their own that legislators had to take action.

Now the inhabitants of the present are now completely surrounded by the legal and electromagnetic equivalent of a barbed-wire jungle, on the other side of which throng the anguished, raging multitudes, their messages smoldering in their bellies, forever undeliverable.

*

XIII

In this realm, nobody pauses to savor a sip of ale, for there are other brews waiting to be sampled. Nobody listens to a melody more than once, for there is other music waiting to be heard. Every conversation is as succinct as possible, for who knows what other equally intriguing person might be about to walk by?

Though a visitor might assume that the realm's inhabitants are born with existential tapeworms, this is not the case—rather, everybody is occupied with preparing for the suspended, seemingly endless moment just prior to death when one re-experiences everything down to the presence of a semicolon in a poem where a lesser writer would have plunked down a mere period, a sprinkling of cumin in a chocolate truffle instead of the more plebian cinnamon or nutmeg. In that moment one can, at last, immerse oneself in sensation, plumbing its depths.

Thus, to proceed through life at a leisurely pace or to return to any particular type of experience is to set oneself up for an impoverished reprise—unthinkable not only for one's own sake but for that of one's heirs, since the entire accumulation is released with the final breath to be inhaled by the near-and-dear, or near-and-dear-enough. A slow-liver or a repeat-sensationist is considered to be a reprobate, guilty of willful negligence; even the coroner refrains from approaching the corpse until the cleanup crew has blasted the area with their power blowers.

*

This realm's entire religious practice is carried out by the committee responsible for compiling a list of everything that's too near to be perceived.

Because all the committee members are chain smokers, though this is not, in fact, a job requirement, the air is so densely blue that their voices seem disembodied, suspended, creating a sense of simultaneous intimacy and buoyancy.

And what is too near to be perceived?

"Heaven," says one voice.

"Ignorance," says a second.

"No, stupidity," another contradicts.

The list grows, is slashed and truncated, remains static for decades, and then begins to sprout again as items are debated, tabled, re-introduced, and then re-contested.

Is its size fixed or potentially infinite?

No one knows; it is not that kind of list.

*

XV

In this realm, a book or newspaper is good for only one-time use, since the reader's gaze actually absorbs the letters and illustrations.

The very poor, known derogatorily as "after-readers," must make do by rummaging in the dumpsters of the well-off in order to scavenge boring descriptive passages the previous reader had skipped or skimmed. Everyone feels sorry for them because they never get any pornography at all.

*

Foreigners in this realm find themselves grateful to the point of near-hysteria that the Tourists' Aid Society has provided mud huts where one may regain equilibrium by staring at the dull, sloping walls; here the landscapes, the people, and even the buildings are so radiantly gorgeous that without such relief, visitors would plummet headlong into psychosis.

The citizens, however, due to either genetic immunity or lifelong exposure, don't register the glory as anything noteworthy, but instead, consider these strangers to be tragically aesthetically challenged.

*

XVII

In this realm of the double births, first comes the infant, scalp creamy with vernix, eyes squeezed shut, and then the shadow that has nourished it throughout gestation, pale at first, but destined to darken with maturity.

The baby is taken home to its bassinet, the shadow to its tank where it slowly expands either in solitude or with the shadows of the siblings. (The failure of these shadows to occasionally indulge themselves in a watery fight over territory, like clashing devil rays, signifies that the siblings have not fully bonded.) Respectable parents change the tank water every morning; careless folk may let it go for several days, allowing it to become murky and pre-toxic.

As soon as a shadow becomes ripe and extended, ready to outgrow its confines, the parents siphon it into a tall ceremonial glass. Its owner, now an adolescent, drinks it down at one sitting, and from then on leaks darkness with every step, a sensation as exhilarating as it is disturbing.

On rare occasions, however, a shadow becomes blighted, or its young person involuntarily regurgitates it. Then the parents roll it into a narrow tube and inter it in a designated graveyard. The shadow's owner, who never loses the glow of childhood, and whose body never attempts to slough off its own image in the sunlight, remains in the family's care, incapable of that sustained creative aggression without which it is impossible to forge a way in the world.

*

XVIII

In this realm, after decades of debate over the fixity vs. the plasticity of human nature, a group of scientists invented a time machine for the sole purpose of stealing an infant from the dawn of the human race in order to observe it in a contemporary environment. Despite the protests of ethicists and historical preservationists, emissary after emissary was sent to the past, but each returned not only empty-handed, but wounded, even maimed.

The public marveled: How problematic could it be to pilfer a prehistoric baby? Not problematic, it turned out: impossible. Those long-ago mothers proved themselves to have been a ferocious bunch in defending their offspring from marauding mountain lions, sizable birds of prey, and the downtrodden graduate students designated for the kidnapping, or, as it was euphemistically called, the "retrieval."

By the fifth failed expedition, funding was running out, and so, under pressure to come up with some—any!—definitive statement, the project leaders declared that human nature had indeed changed, as demonstrated not by the hoped-for infant, but rather by the decrease in maternal competence over time

*

XIX

In this realm, each newborn undergoes a series of ultrasound scans so that the nascent death within might be identified. The parents cherish these milky transparencies, and when the children grow big enough to go to school, they share the ribbon-adorned albums with their classmates. The teachers encourage everyone to honor each death, no matter how awkward or ungainly it may be, so that the child whose image is shaped like a stunted octopus feels no less valued than the child whose image seems to bear the involutions of a rose.

As the children complete their educations and begin pairing off, every lover is drawn not only to the other's appearance, gait, and manner of speaking, but to that one's death as well, pulsing within their embraces.

*

XX

In this realm, reading is the most honorable of all activities, for everybody shares the need to regularly take refuge in a mind other than one's own. No one knows what anyone else is reading, however, since to either ask for or disclose that information would represent the most barbarous of violations. Thus, all books are protected by identical blank covers, and all are the same size—a novella, for instance, is padded with empty pages to keep it from being identified as such—and only members of the booksellers' guild know the citizens' literary tastes.

Even spouses must never cross this boundary—to suggest such a perversion would constitute uncontestable grounds for separation, and besides, every couple knows that there is nothing more erotic than lying side-by-side in bed, each fantasizing about what the other might be reading. That's why in this realm the divorce and literacy rates remain inversely proportional.

*

XXI

There is only one form of entertainment in this realm: self-impersonation contests. So exacting are the judges at these events that though many participants attain low-level awards recognizing various aspects of their performances—timing, execution, etc.—only once or twice in any generation does a competitor walk away with a trophy.

*

XXII

In this realm, the departed are interred face-down, open-eyed, for it is believed that the dark rays of their collective gaze nourish the deep layers of the earth, its hidden springs and passages, the slow, uncoiling currents of its night.

Were their mental concentration to be diminished by even an iota, the underworld would collapse, sucking down the entire surface where the living spend most of their time ferociously napping, cultivating their slumber as other societies do their economies, in hopes of accumulating memories of sleep to console them in their afterlife of vigilance.

*

XXIII

According to this realm's obstetric theory, not only is it not in the least uncommon to find oneself "a little bit pregnant," it is the normal condition of most sexually active fertile women, since the residents of the before-life want to keep their options open, and therefore pay strict attention to every nuance and fluctuation of actual terrestrial existence. What's the current heat index? How's the stock market looking? Are there any good movies out this season, and if not, does the lack of them portend a long-term dip in the quality of popular entertainment? Are seat belts holding during accidents? How many vacationers have suffered shark bites in the last several months? Does this would-be mother like to play loud music at all hours? Does that potential father's family of origin possess a history of calamitous feuds? Compared to those who are trying to decide whether or not to be born, the most fastidious elderly curmudgeon seems a model of affability. And thus, in the realm of vacillating impendence, the pre-born are understood to be forever changing their minds—testing out the climates of various wombs, making their presences known by generating a little queasiness, a prickling of gooseflesh, then retreating into the before-world in much the same way a cautious swimmer will dip a toe into a chilly lake only to pull it back. One might think that this sense of prolonged indeterminacy would annoy the women, but in fact, most of them are not unsympathetic, being occasionally of more than one mind themselves about the prospect of hosting, painfully expelling, and bearing full responsibility for a stranger.

After a birth does occur, the mother gazes into her infant's eyes with fathomless fellow-feeling, for it has chosen to die to countless could-have-beens in order to take the plunge into a single enfleshed particularity.

*

In the language of this realm, there are so many words for "knowledge" that they comprise an enormous collaborative document-in-progress referred to as "The Lexicon." There is a term for knowledge one pretends to possess as well as for knowledge one pretends to not possess, which is not precisely the same as knowledge one is glad to not possess or wishes one possessed; there is a term for knowledge ignored or disregarded; and for anachronistic knowledge, which is related but not equivalent to incongruent knowledge, and very different from extinct knowledge; for knowledge one feels one must protect, as opposed to knowledge by which one feels protected; for useless or unusable knowledge that occupies valuable space in the brain; and for knowledge that is valid but cannot be proven. In this dictionary, you can find words for knowledge that is exothermic and endothermic; stillborn or still-forming; disfigured or disintegrating; heavy, light, and weightless; knowledge to which someone significant to the bearer is oblivious; symbiotic (not the same as parasitic) knowledge; merely local knowledge; mutating, expanding, and contracting knowledge of many varieties.

"The Lexicon" is not, of course, merely a book, but rather, an archival coral reef of ever-evolving elucidation that occupies over half of the capital city's office buildings. This is why the realm has never pursued expansionist foreign policies— why bother, when the people already possess such a far-flung definitional frontier? And this is why the national religion is the quest for "what escapes" or "what [uncontainably] overflows/ brims over"—by which they mean that particular variety of knowledge impossible to label or categorize. Though nobody can imagine what this might turn out to be, the citizens agree that they will be able to identify it by its conspicuous absence from The Lexicon on The Day of Completion when the final entry has been inscribed. But how are they to know when this occurs? In government conference rooms throughout the realm, teams of federally-appointed theologians argue around the clock over how to even begin to determine such a thing.

Working against this entire enterprise, however, are the Antidefinitionists, those zealots who have sworn blood oaths to dismantle, disassemble, and disarticulate The Lexicon itself.

Though their numbers are few, the realm maintains a sizeable standing army of combat-trained librarians to guard The Lexicon's enormous embossed pages from stealth attacks, any one of which could set the whole endeavor back several generations.

*

In this realm, it is everyone's task to maintain each other's visibility by granting the recommended daily amount of privacy, since people begin to disappear in bits and pieces when they are deprived of sufficient time alone.

Newborns are, of course, one hundred percent visible, having been cloistered within protective uterine walls throughout gestation, but social workers patrol the streets, keeping an eye out for any child with a translucent elbow, transparent ear, or missing hand—in many cases, a portion of the lost or vanishing body part can be restored by solitude therapeutically administered in foster care, but sometimes, sadly, it is too late, and the individual remains stuck in some stage of invisibility for the rest of his or her life.

By law, every public venue reserves seats for the Full Invisibles who, as a mark of minority pride, eschew the clothing that would establish for others their locations in space.

*

XXVI

This realm houses the world-famous Institute to which so many people make pilgrimage that the border officials don't even bother to ask travelers their purpose, but instead, simply hand them directions to the Institute's front gate.

With all these would-be entreatants, the halls and chambers of the Institute should be crowded, even claustrophobic, but this is far from the case. Have the visitors gotten lost in the city, been waylaid by local lowlife, or slipped from the famous National Marble Bridge into the river below?

No, they can be found in the Institute gardens, sitting or napping on benches beneath the vine-covered trellises, indefinitely prolonging the very condition they have traveled here to reverse. When they were home, fretting over their strayed memories and evaporated insights, they threw all of their energies into the project of attaining visas, but now, having at last arrived at The Institute of Lost Thoughts, they find themselves reluctant to go in, though it is a simple matter to extricate their vanished mental states from the steaming sea of cerebral activity that sloshes inside the human skull—a few moments under the scanners, a brief consultation with the clinical staff, and there you'd be at the out-take station, holding the printed version of those particular ideas you'd feared you might never again encounter.

But what if it turns out that their quality, clarity, originality, and overall preciousness fail to equal the intensity of your desire for them? Might not the loss you'd endured up until that moment have been more bearable—in fact, more pleasurable—than such a let-down?

That is why so many visitors take up permanent residence in the gardens, nibbling on the fruits and pastries proffered by the ever-solicitous vendors, and sleeping under the fragrant bushes.

And that is why the gardens are perpetually expanding, threatening to overrun the National Post Office, the National Mint, and the National Egg-Processing Facility, while the Institute itself shrinks as the trustees declare various sections closed until further notice in order to cut maintenance expenses.

*

In this realm, citizens remain veiled at all times. Infants' faces are covered immediately after birth so that everyone grows up perceiving the world through a fine silk mesh

Of course, things weren't always this way. According to the national myth, everyone went around bare-faced until one night at the winter feast, a bard sang a poignant ballad about two lovers who exchanged their lonelinesses by gazing into one another's eyes. The bard's tale had been metaphorical, not literal, but since in this population, as in most others, literal thinkers outnumber metaphorical thinkers by at least 500 to 1, all kinds of people immediately engaged in that same exchange, some with the ones they most cherished, and others with the nearest individuals at hand. And it didn't stop there. Because each person found the new loneliness so unbearably alien and excruciatingly familiar, everyone rushed to seek relief through another exchange, and then another and another in a web of bewildering transpositions. Ironically, every soul longed for his or her original loneliness as if for a vanished beloved, and thus, art and the alphabet sprang into existence prematurely and under great pressure in this realm as citizens strove to depict the densities, textures, etc. of their original conditions. Very occasionally, a loneliness would be restored to its birth-host, but after the extended trauma of separation, the fit never felt quite right. Even more rarely, a loneliness would inexplicably reject a host, or vice versa. Those disembodied lonelinesses wandered throughout the realm seeking some altruist to take them in, though the highest number of concurrent lonelinesses anyone survived was, purportedly, three.

To restore order, the people agreed to don veils. And eventually, of course, everyone who had participated in these exchanges passed away, replaced by a generation that knew about them only second-hand. Now, centuries later, tourists are drawn to this realm, imagining that any society so obsessed with veils must be exotic, but they almost always leave long before their visas have expired, repelled by the culture of personal distance.

*

XXVIII

Immediately after a birth in this realm, a team of clinicians gathers to tabulate the newborn's margins of error while the family waits in the reception area, not infrequently in such a state of collective anxiety that the attending nurse must administer sedatives.

An across-the-board wide-margined set of results inspires all kinds of festivities; in years to come, when this individual is seen skateboarding down the street, embarking on a romance, charbroiling meat in the back yard, or enlisting in the military, no one will worry, since the usual human blunders will bring about only limited consequences.

Everyone knows, however, what devastation a narrowly-margined person can wreak across the generations through one extra drink, one episode of jaywalking, one ill-advised fling, one slipup with a calculator. Thus, a set of narrow margins is cause for solemn strategic planning. The family divests itself of all fragile, expensive, or potentially dangerous possessions—the stove must be uprooted and banished, so that all food may be brought in from the outside, tested, and then fed to the individual in tiny portions; the elegant, angular wooden furniture must be exchanged for padded blobs of chairs and bulbous rubber tables; and helmets and shin guards must be ordered from special catalogues. These changes represent only the beginning of a seemingly endless set of arrangements which include all manner of personal guardians, chaperones, and tutelary figures, not merely for the individual, but for all of the other family members, each of whose well-being is endangered by this person's very existence. The entire group endures dolorously, as though beneath a pall. Neighbors move away, and property values plummet.

Both of the above descriptions represent extremes, of course. Most people are born with a mixed set of margins for error—wide in cards, romance and academics, for instance, narrower in finances, and average in employment and physical exertions. These indicators cause neither panic nor celebration, but rather, a steady, moderate attention to various kinds of risk prevention.

According to ancient prophecies, a day will dawn when everyone's margins begin to spontaneously and randomly widen or narrow. Skeptics scoff at this notion; believers argue with each other about whether there is any point in attempting to prepare for such a massive disruption; and many remain more or less agnostic, but most people find themselves at least occasionally yearning for the event to occur, since the prophecy mandates that after the pandemonium subsides and margins return to their fixed, predictable condition, a year-long period of public grace must ensue during which all contracts, from marriage to real estate to employment, may be dissolved or reinstituted without penalty.

*

XXIX

In this realm, labor is compensated in inverse proportion to its tangibility.

Just after dawn today, the theoretician who calculates the fluctuating sizes of various potential infinities breakfasted on lobster and vintage Bordeaux, and members of the Southern New Jersey Jazz Composers Collective climbed into private jets for their quarterly professional conference on their own resort archipelago, while the construction engineer, under whose direction rises a suspension bridge that will forever alter ecosystems and traffic patterns, attempted to quiet his stomach on a leftover heel of bread charred in his electrically unstable thrift-store toaster while he scanned the classifieds for weekend work scrubbing the floors of lyric poets.

*

XXX

Because here every generation aspires to bring forth more children than did the previous one, there are so many people in this realm of accelerating congestion that events seem to transpire almost simultaneously. Convergence is the rule, and coincidence the norm, so that a dinner party turns out to be remarkable when several guests don't discover that they were born the same hour of the same day in the same hospital, just as a fender-bender is deemed astonishing when it doesn't bring about the reunion of kindergarten sweethearts or some such occurrence. Nearly smothered with correspondences, everyone suffers from a surfeit of signification, yearning for the inevitable moment when the realm's data finally reaches critical mass, information begins to flow backward toward dissolution, and the soul can at last find rest in the inconsequential.

*

Question: What do the following inhabitants of this realm, strangers to one another, have in common?

a. the scholar shredding his dissertation
b. the scientist scowling at the printout of her test results
c. the songwriter unable to move past the first stanza

Answer: Each has neglected to maintain payments for Individual Epiphany Insurance, allowing coverage to lapse. Thus, despite the severity of their woes, no one will offer them even the most perfunctory expression of sympathy.

*

XXXII

Before a new year may begin in this realm, all the families are confined to their homes in order to adjust accounts as everyone contends for his or her version of the previous year.

Imagine a bleary mother peeking out from a crack between the curtains at all the residents of her village who, having completed their own calculations, now wait on her lawn, picnicking in the snow on savory roast turkey. Her family has been re-breathing each others' air for the past week-and-a-half, and most of the food they'd stored for this ordeal has been consumed; it is up to her, she realizes, to take strategic advantage of their fatigue and hunger in order to push through to resolution.

So she turns back to the little group huddled in their bathrobes around the fireplace, and begins what she hopes will be the final round by proposing a particular configuration that she has been keeping up her sleeve: the father will have to give up his version of the incident at the beach last summer in exchange for the eldest daughter's, and the daughter will have to sacrifice her interpretation of the recent birthday party debacle for that of the second son, who will come out slightly ahead of the others regarding instances of acquiescence, but slightly behind in terms of their intensity. Since the children are at a deadlock over who is to blame for the unlatched gate/ missing puppy tragedy, and none has accumulated enough credits to out-bargain or out-buy the others, they will liquidate their individual invention capital to collaborate on a new version on which they can agree.

Though all are astonished at the mother's finesse and fortitude, she is careful to appear dispassionate, for this is the most delicate of junctures; if none of the stipulations suffers defeat, the family might even now be just on the verge of finalizing their reality contract so that collective time can once more lurch into motion.

*

XXXIII

If you were to find yourself in this realm, you'd probably spend your first few days trying to identify what it is about its culture that makes you uneasy, as though you were perpetually stumbling at the bottom of a familiar staircase that has inexplicably and without warning become a half-step too short. "What could it be?" you'd keep asking yourself. Sooner or later, it would dawn on you that this is a society completely devoid of metaphor: there are no figures of speech, no symbolic or referential constructions of word or image—nothing is perceived as being like anything else, but rather, everything is merely, and stolidly, itself. No matter where you looked, you would find no poignancy, melancholy, irony, theology, advertising, house pets, forbidden longings, or mortuary science.

"How flat, how drab, how sad," you'd think, and so you'd become a metonymic missionary, forcing tropes into every conversation in hopes that they would spread like spores through the region, but the natives would respond to your efforts with such a courtesy of incomprehension that you'd slip into a funk, speaking only when necessary, all the while wondering what kind of genetic neural short-circuiting had stunted this realm's cognitive development.

Eventually, however, you would start to second-guess this assessment. What if, in this realm's distant past, its inhabitants had experienced the world in the same analogical manner as your people presently do, but at some point had transcended the need to process their perception through acts of association? Because you could not come up with any possible way to prove or disprove this hypothesis, its presence in your mind would torment you; even after returning home, you'd remain forever obsessed with the notion that everyone there is gazing cleanly into the essence of things while you yourself glimpse only distortions through the muddy turmoil of your primitive brain.

*

XXXIV

In this realm, though the first groups of vacationers to the past had conscientiously refrained from the import and export of deodorant tubes, miniature flasks of absinthe, etc., they unwittingly carried into previous centuries all kinds of viruses against which the natives had no immunities, so that history's dead soon far outnumbered its living, many of whom were conscripted to dig mass graves.

The generation of the travelers was aware that their continuing existence represented the ultimate logical incongruity, since most of their ancestors had perished long before they themselves had been conceived, but apparently, there was a fair amount of wiggle room in these matters. Nevertheless, physicists warned that a delayed reaction might ensue, causing the past to collapse in on itself, drawing the present and the future down with it.

So they decided to repopulate history. Citizens were deployed according to their estimated compatibility with destination eras; although there was an initial attempt to keep families together, unpleasant decisions had to be made and enforced; after all, wasn't reality itself at stake? After the departures, each time-border was sealed to prevent further disasters from occurring, and now there they all were, locked into their assigned chronological zones, which, including the "new present," were as yet quite sparsely inhabited.

It was clear to everyone that both the trauma and the opportunity were unprecedented. While not a few individuals were thrilled with this chance to start over (these were on the lam from various predicaments they had created for themselves in the "old present"), most others found themselves careening between numbness, gut-grinding grief, and a nearly manic pioneering enthusiasm, scarcely knowing what to make of themselves, let alone their extraordinary new environments.

And how did they begin to adjust? By telling stories, each of which began with the statement: "And nothing was ever the same before that."

*

XXX

Immediately upon awakening in this realm, everyone checks his or her personal reality quotient. Basic, primary-level aliveness is identified by the presence of breath on glass, the inability to walk backward through mirrors, and so on, but these are only the first of many self-administered tests regarding various subtle levels of being and non-existence.

The chores of the day are then divvied up according to the results. Those with high reality quotients take responsibility for the duties demanding focused presence and attention— they care for the young; diagnose and treat the ill; and create, interpret, and enforce public policy. Those who registered low are set to sweeping the streets and stocking the shelves of shops, performing those chores that can be accomplished mostly "on automatic." Paradoxically, the citizens who tested hyper-real share in this work; because even their most mundane experiences are pyrotechnically vivid, such tasks represent the outside limit of what they can bear.

Those whose test scores fell on the negative end of the continuum become, for that day, salespeople, news forecasters, sports announcers, and disc jockeys; they are best-suited to absorbing and transmitting the energies of others, as they have less than none of their own.

*

XXXVI

No two people in this realm are allowed to marry without first pledging the collateral of their single worst characteristics.

This arrangement remains merely an abstraction unless the couple attempts to separate, at which point each individual experiences a double anguish: the shocking loss of that familiar personal flaw, and the intolerable intrusion of the partner's foible ("It felt like a lead ball the size of a grapefruit had been forcibly inserted into my spleen," commented one would-be ex-spouse).

Having directly experienced each other's inner territory, most couples end up not only reconciling but enjoying a new mutual empathy. The ones who divorce, on the other hand, despise each other all the more. Their rancor seethes and roils, emitting invisible toxic fumes. Thus, life proceeds with about the same amount of well-being and misery as in the other realms, though in rather more concentrated portions.

*

XXXVII

Behold, an infant has just been born into silence. Even while in the womb, it has heard no human speech, for in this realm, all pregnant women go to a resort where everyone refrains from speaking, even to herself. And now the obstetrical team attends to the mother and child, communicating through a sign language comprised of the appropriate medical terminology. The mother is beaming, not in adoration of the infant, whom she may never see again, but because she is about to return to the world of chatter, soliloquy, and song.

In a few hours, the baby will be whisked to one of the many cottages scattered across the countryside. Though a professional nurse will give it as much goat's milk and affection as it desires, she will never utter a single word in its presence. Thus free of all external influence, the young one's cooings and babblings will naturally begin to evolve into the particular linguistic patterns by which its true clan may be identified; once kinship is established, the child will straightaway be united with its people in this happiest of realms where everyone lives amongst those with whom he or she actually belongs.

*

In this realm, after you have been yourself for a sufficient amount of time to establish your identity, you may request to be someone else for a while.

Your petition will be evaluated in the light of all the other such applications—if too many were granted simultaneously, the realm's consciousness would tip, becoming either wholly collective or wholly individual instead of teetering between the two states.

Of course, while you are being someone else, on sabbatical from your own life, that person or some other is being you, indulging in your pleasures and, as if on safari, braving your nightmares.

Once in a while, one of those rare individuals with an unusually capacious soul will vacation at a site meant for someone smaller (like squeezing oneself into a pup tent during a camping expedition—not all that unpleasant in the short run, and certainly worth it for the scenery), leaving space for a double occupancy so that two people can share it, cabin mates on the cruise of an irreducible human soul.

*

XXXIX

Every year in this realm as the snow drifts start to unravel, the inhabitants bustle about stockpiling canned goods and cutting wood to board up their windows, for with the change of seasons come the dreaded, utterly silent free-will winds, which sweep in over the mountains like herds of velvet-shod horses.

This is a society so dedicated to the cultivation of courage that their toddlers are taught to log wrestle (parents line the river banks, their harsh cries urging the little ones on toward feats of intensifying ferocity). Yet no one braves even the least breath of these winds. And who would not commend such caution? What soul could hope to recover from glimpsing—even for an instant—everything of which it is capable?

*

XL

In this realm, women give birth in cemeteries to honor the dead and keep them where they belong; it is believed that a birth in any other site would provoke them to leave their graves and hunt down the child and miscreant mother. The system satisfies everyone—the babies because they don't know any better; the dead because their hospitality is appreciated; and the mothers because all the cemeteries are equipped with the most contemporary obstetrical apparatus; it doesn't seem macabre to anyone that the fathers' video cameras capture not only the infants' silky crowning scalps but the nearby headstones, and that the lamps illumine epitaphs as well as the little weighing scales. The tightly laced boughs of the great cemetery trees provide shade and protection from the rain, and so many plants breathe along the pathways that it is as if each baby is drawing its first breath inside a great and glowing greenhouse.

*

XLI

In this realm, small children remain unnamed, and are not considered fully "born" until their first attempt at deception, generally around the age of three, because only then is the child's soul sufficiently engaged with the world to experience the urge to contradict, negate, or re-imagine it. The incident is duly inscribed in its appropriate spot in the realm's detailed taxonomy of first lies, and a name is assigned to the child based on some saint or hero whose first lie fell into the same category—some highly specific subset of "blame-aversion, " for instance, or "task-avoidance." Once every hundred years or so, a lie is designated as authentically unclassifiable, so with great hoopla, the creation of a new category is announced, and the child is given an original name.

Even more infrequently, a child grows up without lying, or at least, without ever being caught. This individual proceeds through life nameless and revered, for the populace is neither particularly dishonest nor particularly fanciful, and there is almost no crime or fiction in this realm of the late-born liars.

*

XLII

Every adult occasionally experiences cloudy, disturbing dreams of this realm because each has spent a season there in Suffering School.

Though it is common knowledge that some two-thirds of the alumni will not retain the skills learned here, at the close of term, each class must demonstrate the ability to distinguish monotony from loneliness, loneliness from hunger, hunger from fatigue, fatigue from irritation, irritation from lust, and so on. Each class must be able to identify the common types of temporal suffering, from the mildest, such as being obligated to keep pace with someone much slower than oneself, to the most extreme, such as being forced to inhale time contaminated by exposure to excessive velocity and torque. The higher-level students are challenged to demonstrate cellular flexion within pain structures of variable increments and durations.

Only the finest, however, are tested in the advanced arts of vicarious suffering and the transmission of healing to past and future generations. And each term, only two or three superlative students prove worthy to undergo the examination determining whether they can endure actual delight.

*

XLIII

According to popular belief in this realm, each home and business possesses, or rather, is possessed by, a designated ghost responsible for providing the particular instances of disruption and contradiction it deems pertinent to the situations at hand. When selling a house, one is legally bound to disclose the ghost's idiosyncrasies along with those of the heating/ventilation systems.

These ghosts are not, of course, exempt from ageing. Of all discarnate entities, a young or elderly ghost is assumed to behave most like a pet—antic or sedate—to the point of sleeping invisibly curled up with the cats and dogs, sharing their wicker baskets or smelly, fur-covered blankets. A middle-aged ghost, on the other hand, is expected to remain professional in its demeanor almost to the point of emotional disengagement even while performing its most trickster-like machinations—a good thing, too, since its mind is undoubtedly elsewhere, preoccupied with its own mid-death crisis.

When a ghost passes away, it observes (with satisfaction, chagrin, or indifference, as may be the case) its otherworldly memorial ceremony, and then reincarnates as an infant ghost. Instead of transmigrating with it, its memories automatically appear as a set of volumes in the enormous and ever-expanding phantasmal library where they are perused to about the same degree as the corporeal reading public absorbs the biographies of its former citizens. Thus, the amount of reading material in the after-world is said to far surpass the number of actual readers, a situation which may be considered heavenly or hellish, according to individual taste.

*

XLIV

Just before sundown on the last day of every year, a helicopter flies in over this floating island, and like a bulky, clattering angel bestowing manna from heaven, releases through its hatch a rubbery shower of all the erasers that have been used and discarded by the other regions. Though these darkened stumps represent the realm's only permissible artistic medium, there are no other works in the world whose expressive qualities equal those of these masterpieces, all rendered in exquisite blacks and grays.

When the island cannot be located by radar, and the helicopter must fly low over the various contiguous oceans and seas to seek it, the citizens of the other realms seem to hold their breaths, exhaling only when the loudspeakers announce that the year's accumulated smudges, smears, and repentances have been safely delivered to their designated afterlife.

*

XLV

In this realm, people take turns being old, passing the condition around like a sacred chalice or a hot potato. As with jury duty, no one must endure it for very long, but no one is exempt. The elderly are treated with respectful tenderness, since today's senior citizen, who may not recognize her own child, will soon remember all too well the fact that a neighbor took advantage of her hesitant pace, inserting himself before her in the cafeteria line.

Though the realm's collectivism does not extend to the phenomenon of death, according to legend, this was not always so; when there were only enough people to fill a few small villages, everyone took turns being dead, so that during any given season, about a third of the inhabitants would be laid out in the underground caverns that honeycomb the region, while the rest of the villagers scurried about their business, making up for lost time.

No one is certain how this equitable arrangement ended. Some say that the larger the population grew, the more difficult and complicated the rotation became until it was finally abandoned altogether; others claim that a particular group refused to take their turn in the caverns, disrupting the process; still others speculate that in fact the reverse was the case, and that some of the dead began refusing to return. Was this because the afterlife was so very delightful or because the earthly life was so very disagreeable? Historians can only guess, since all records of that era have long since been lost—or, as some maintain, suppressed; conspiracy theories abound, but no one takes them seriously, not even the ones who circulate them, since the annual brush with old age, which begins in the thirty-fifth year of life, has impressed upon the national character a noticeable equanimity, or, as some outsiders claim, a fatalism.

XLV

In this realm, when the behavior of a citizen becomes chronically difficult, that individual is sent back to the previous life stage, advancing again from that point until he or she has reworked the personality characteristics in question.

For instance, nobody thinks it at all unusual for a truculent teenager to become an eleven-year-old again, experiencing a respite from emotional volatility, and then beginning to experience the early throes of adolescence for the second time while retaining the memories of already having lived through the ages of twelve, thirteen, and fourteen. As a rule, the former teenager's schoolmates are significantly sobered by this spectacle, and it rarely takes more than one such regression to bring an entire group of troublemakers to order.

However, when the difficult person is much older, all kinds of brain-wave tests must be administered in order to determine whether the individual is authentically suffering a personality disruption rather than merely faking one in order to be made younger for a while.

*

XLVII

In this realm, every newborn is given a name of many syllables set to musical tones, which then shrinks by a tone or two a year to honor the fact that the more deeply one knows a person, the more mysterious he or she becomes. Thus, the longest intimacies are acknowledged by songs composed of the most luxuriant silence.

*

XLVIII

Lined up at the registry office in this realm, the pairs of young lovers shift and jitter in a long, fraying wave. They are of age, or have received parental permission to marry; they have passed their blood tests; they are carrying proof that they possess visible means of support. The way before them is clear save for the last, most crucial verification.

The door opens, and a couple emerges, grinning, holding hands, blinking back bright tears. An exhalation rises from those still waiting—though they are happy for this pair, this set of result signifies that their own chances are now slightly decreased. *Four out of ten don't pass*…the phrase ripples again through the line, for this is the official statistic, though of course, that's in total over the *entire population*—it doesn't mean, they reassure each other, four out of ten *today*. Nevertheless, the already-clingy sweethearts cling a little more stickily.

And now the next couple steps into the room. The equipment is simple, and the examination painless, but the two are loath to let go of each others' hands in order to step up to the machines for analysis, for if their boredoms do not register as displaying the requisite compatibility level, the marriage license will be denied, and each of the lovers will have to either seek a different mate or live alone forever.

Or will they? Some whisper about a secret underground comprised of lovers who suspect that the internal landscape is capable of being—well, landscaped—shaped, sculpted—that innate boredom style may be, if not transformed, at least modified—that spouses can not only learn to manage boredom incompatibility, but may bond more enduringly for having done so.

Of course, people don't speak of this often—it's best to not dwell on such things—but after a negative test result, the loved ones of the separated would-be soul mates are likely to keep a close collective eye on them, even sweep them off for extended family vacations in remote places, entertaining them so exhaustively that they can't help but fall asleep each night too numb and weary to contemplate scenarios everyone knows are possible only in legends.

*

XLIX

One day, historians announced their discovery that at some point far back in this realm's history, a Great Dilution had occurred (perhaps gradually, perhaps all at once), causing everything to diminish in vividness and intensity by precisely 23 percent.

Even ordinary water, famous for tasting like nothing at all, was apparently now releasing only 77 percent of the flavor of nothing.

Was it reality itself that had changed, or merely the people's ability to perceive it?—or was there, in fact, any distinction between these two possibilities? No one had any idea. And when the initial flurry of reactions to the news had subsided, most people went along just as they had before—after all, the event in question had taken place a very long time ago, so what did it really have to do with them?

Some of the populace were relieved, however; these individuals had always suspected that something was missing, and had engaged in various kinds of frenzied entertainments and exertions in order to compensate. Now they found themselves free to enjoy a 77 percent satisfying breath of reprieve. Others were appalled. To them, even "ordinary experience" had already seemed quite excessive, so the phantom 23 percent constituted nothing but threat: if it had inexplicably gone away, it could just as inexplicably return! Now they would have to struggle against not only the 77 percent that had been exhausting them, but their own fear that the very next moment might bring about the bursting-forth of the rest.

What did the people in these two groups have in common? Each had privately assumed that he or she was the only one who'd felt either the deficiency or the excess of existence, and had thus attributed the sensation to some personal (though unidentifiable) flaw.

That is how a new verb phrase came into being, which may be translated as something along the lines of: "to feel at once both a little less isolated and a little less unique."

*

L

Though for the most part everyone here wears flowing silvery garb, as if glass were processed as a textile, this is the least narcissistic of realms, for all other reflecting surfaces are prohibited. When people glimpse their own faces in each others' robes, rather than seeing the preening, posing versions that would show up in private mirrors, they are confronted by the half-sneer no less ugly for its subtlety, the small lie skewing the smile. Thus, the legally mandated fashion of this realm provides immediate feedback inspiring, for the most part, instant self-correction.

The only citizens exempt from wearing the robes are those responsible for caring for infants, who cannot begin to form anything like a "self" without first having experienced the "other" as self; new lovers and the newly bereaved, whose sense of self is in violent flux; and, for obvious reasons, the walking dead. All of these can be seen around town in the traditional cottons, linens, wools, and, of course, the standard stained-and-winding grave clothes.

*

If you ventured into this realm, you might come to the conclusion that some glutinous quantum substance had leaked into the mechanism of time and then hardened—everywhere around you, you'd see individuals inexplicably freezing in place for a short while, and then resuming their activities as though no interruption had occurred. You might conduct your affairs here with some trepidation, awaiting the sensation of your own muscles beginning to lock down, but you'd soon learn that these episodes are wholly voluntary. This is the parenthetical realm, where it is considered inappropriate to move directly from one experience to the next without an interval during which to cleanse the soul's palate, so to speak. Were you to ask the inhabitants what they are actually "doing" during these motionless periods, you wouldn't receive any satisfactory answers, for this "between" state is, by definition, indeterminate. (It is widely believed that these caesuras are not even deducted from one's lifespan, though how could such a notion either be verified or refuted?)

Often, visitors return to their own realms zealous to introduce this custom, but apart from the community context, they soon abandon the enterprise, which becomes a memory no less wistful for its vagueness.

*

LII

Here every adult is afforded the opportunity to approach death in a sequence that is largely self-determined.

A few citizens choose to immediately relinquish the faculties they most value—for them, the initial sacrifice is often the entire sense of sight or hearing, or even the ability to recognize loved ones. According to these stoics (or, as some call them, "show-offs"), this is not unlike jumping into the deep end of a pool instead of inching and squealing one's way from the shallow end.

Others behave as though they are engaging in an enforced striptease, giving up as little as possible along the way until they are left with nothing to let go of but what they believe makes them who they are. These are the ones who offer up such items as sensation in the left pinkie toenail or the ability to hear a type of music they have always detested.

Most of the realm's inhabitants, however, forego their option to choose. They prefer the possibility of, say, early paralysis or dementia to the choice between performing supererogatory exploits of capitulation to their own mortality or (as they see it) wasting their remaining days in petty calculation and computation. In a dark inversion of giving birth, they don't want to know the details ahead of time, but would rather be "surprised."

*

LIII

Though there is no consensus on who started the trouble—the unmarried, the orphans, the surviving siblings of deceased twins?—it is evident to all that the situation has gotten quite out of hand. Citizens overflow the court rooms, petitioning for official emancipation from their kin in order to join the new clan composed entirely of the realm's solitaries.

*

At the end of this realm's first week of mind travel, the government announced that it had been secretly tracking everyone's cognitive comings and goings. Almost without exception, people had voyaged into one another's thoughts primarily for the purpose of visiting their own images there— not only in order to "see" how their neighbors "saw" them, but to revise and re-sculpt these versions of themselves. While everyone was enjoying the collective glow of this delightful and mostly spurious mutual regard, the entire society was in danger of slipping through the gap between the real and the re-styled—how many of the more unscrupulous sort, for instance, had already begun to whitewash their images in the thoughts of their crime victims?

Mental travel was immediately suspended while the legislators convened. After many hours of deliberation, they enacted a magnificently airtight anti-vandalism law: all the alterations must be reversed, and from now on, no one would be permitted to even touch, let alone tamper with, his or her own image in the brain of another. Penalties for infringement were so severe that nobody would dare risk incurring them, and so, happily for all, the travel could begin again.

For a time everything seemed to be going so smoothly that a few neighboring realms even began to consider making mind-travel available to their citizens. Before long, however, it became clear that a new peril had arisen. Though the people dutifully refrained from manipulating their neighbors' mental impressions of them, the new law did not prevent looking, and that's what they did, completely consumed with ogling the various versions of themselves in each other's brains. Interestingly, these mental travelers proved no less titillated by the ugly, even distorted versions of themselves than they were by the flattering ones. Since nobody wanted to do anything so comparatively dull as bother with normal daily tasks, the infrastructure was swiftly unraveling. The council met again, banning any and all forms of mental tourism.

Historians now universally consider that original week of mind travel to have been the realm's true (albeit necessarily brief) golden age. Indeed, a certain residual cheerfulness still lingers amongst the populace even as each citizen chafes under permanent house arrest in his or her solitary brain.

*

LV

In this realm where each clan's speech bears almost no resemblance to that of its neighbors, the most highly-esteemed individuals are the philological physicians who treat the various languages after they have undergone the daily wrackings, gougings, sievings, churnings, palpations, and wringings-out—in other words, the daily occasions of interpretation and translation—necessary for commerce.

Because everyone understands that language is an acutely sensitive entity with countless, nearly infinitesimal nerve endings, no one can help but be aware of a personal complicity with the suffering. To be tormented, then gradually, painfully healed only to be tormented again—all for the sake of the economy! What monsters the people know themselves to be! Surely some extreme collective penance must be in order. Yet who can imagine an affliction severe enough to assuage their consciences but tolerable enough to allow business to continue without even a momentary lessening of speed and intensity, let alone (heaven forbid!) an observable interruption?

*

While in other realms people tend to argue about politics or religion, this realm has long been characterized by disputes over the nature of consciousness—so much so, in fact, that a huge portion of the nation's resources has gone into developing deep-brain-sweep technology. When this technology was finally ready, not a single individual declined testing, despite the procedure's migraine-inducing properties.

Then came months of tabulation, correlation, and synthesis while the citizenry speculated about the outcome, neglecting their work in order to configure and reconfigure the betting pools. Since everyone was so sure he or she soon would be proven right regarding pet cognitive issues, the atmosphere was festive—entrepreneurs racked up a tidy sum marketing bumper stickers and t-shirts announcing such propositions as "MY RED IS NOT YOUR ORANGE" and "PERCEPTION: PRIMARILY DISCONTINUOUS!"

But now the clamor has ceased. At every street corner and cafe, people are reading the official results, which fill the entire newspaper, learning that red is indeed the same for everyone; that for a third of the population, the greatest mental pleasure is anticipatory nostalgia; that something about being human feels like metal grinding against metal or bone against bone, since either the body could be bearable or the soul, but together, they are not bearable; that according to the evidence, it's a toss-up as to whether the little stories are coalescing or the one big story is breaking down; that the phenomenon producing the highest intensity of brain-itch is that it is never "you" who dies; that almost universally, the time required for convalescing from happiness increases with age; that certain kinds of forgetting cancel one another out; that no occasion of "getting what you want," "getting what you don't want," and "not getting what you want" is ever actually "over."

Engrossed in their discoveries, these citizens do not realize that they are moments away from comprehending everything about the will, the dream life, and all other such former enigmas. The very instant the slowest reader arrives at the end of the last sentence, this realm will be a land without mystery, all the inhabitants bored out of their minds with mind itself, as if they had decided to give the sea, their ancestral home, a good cleaning, drawing from it with hooks and nets all vestiges of marine life from the cathedral-whale to the dwarf nautilus with its ever-antecedent chambers; innumerable human corpses in various stages of decomposition along with their orphaned coracles, galleons, and supersonic transport jets; the tragically sunken panhandles of old coastlines; and, of course, the shadows of all the above, incommensurately denser than their objects, leaving the ocean empty of everything but water, so shallow that it could no longer be considered, in any sense of the word, "abyssal," having been reduced to something not unlike an overblown wading pool, the treasure cluttering the beaches rendered worthless in this new element of unmitigated transparency.

*

LVII

Whenever a team of traveling evangelists enters this realm to ask passers-by whether or not each has "a personal relationship with God," the response is always a shrug of bemusement. Here, an inhabitant's communications with the Deity are visible to all in a porous, translucent cloud that shimmers just above his or her head but does not show up in mirrors or film; ironically, if you were a native, your only access to your particular cloud would be through the people around you who are, upon your request, obligated to reveal to you these sacred interactions.

Legibility is frequently an issue, however, not to mention reading comprehension, as each individual's cloud hosts a continually shifting multi-dimensional montage of highly personal symbols and images in color combinations as subtle as they are significant. Thus, by the time someone has described to you the contents of your cloud, the information has been filtered once through your reader's consciousness and again through your interpretation of his or her depiction, rendering the results suspect. Some citizens seek increased accuracy by garnering as many readings as possible in the brief period of time before the cloud's contents have altogether changed, whereas others adhere to a theology of single-reader-fidelity. Each method possesses its disadvantages, such as the likelihood of superficial readings if there are many people involved, or on the other hand, the trauma of starting over if your lone reader dies, moves away, or, worst of all, has a falling-out with you, thereby contaminating previous readings in a reverse withdrawal of trust.

Of course, citizens regularly delve into one another's clouds to extricate fragments they find particularly appealing, which then appear, re-contextualized, in their own—every cloud is deemed to be in the public domain, which is why the evangelists tend to return to their own realms bewildered and incoherent—that is, if they return at all.

*

LVIII

In this realm, you can't be truly dead until everyone with whom you've ever interacted has a.) been informed of your new status, and b.) undergone each of the unpredictable, and often recursive, stages of grief. You yourself, of course, are the last to be told, in order that you may remain undistracted and productive throughout the decades it takes for the news of your demise to reach all the long-lost bit-players of your life (who, because they don't even remember you, experience no reaction to speak of), as well as for your near-and-dear to fully mourn you (in secret, so as to not cause you any agitation). That's why most people aren't quite sure whether they're genuinely alive or all-but-officially deceased. If you were a citizen of this realm, you might keep a nervous watch on friends and relations—is your wife rubbing her eyes because, as she claims, she's spent too much time reading in poor light, or is she attempting to camouflage the sorrow of bereavement? On the other hand, you might cruise with insouciance through even your most irksome daily routines, believing yourself likely to be ontologically exempt from the mortal weathers of tedium and vexation.

*

LIX

All artists in this realm labor anonymously, dropping off their works at the Central Depository during the dark of night to be discovered when the citizens arrive at dawn like so many beach-combers looking for ocean treasures brought in by the tide.

Of course, some of these citizens are the artists themselves, lurking near their own pieces to spy on their neighbors as they opine about the still-damp painting or remark upon the freshly written poem.

This arrangement is as close as any realm has come to separating art from ego—another step farther, and there might not be any art at all.

If you lived here, you'd treat everybody you meet with high reverence, since it's not impossible that the seeming-dullard next door secretly penned the play whose intensity all the dramas of the decade will aspire to live up to.

*

LXI

In this realm, most of the citizens have become aficionados of their own death scenes, travelling repeatedly into the future to snap photographs from various angles, host parties, or engage in religious ceremonies whether or not the dying version of any particular self is still a believer.

Anyone who finds the memory of these last moments too unpleasant to bear may have it surgically removed at great expense and considerable physical discomfort. Nine times out of ten, however, immediately upon recovery, the individual feels compelled to make the trip to regain it, despite reading multiple warnings against this written by the pre-surgical self—many unfortunates trap themselves in a perverse cycle of extractions and revelations.

While it is possible to include in one's living will a provision barring all versions of the self from "the demise site," everybody knows that this is merely *pro forma*; what actual power could the dying exercise over all those comparatively healthy younger selves who find such pleasure in debating or attempting to conciliate one another as they jockey for a better view?

*

LXII

In this realm, the ultimate shame is to die beautiful, your face appallingly devoid of furrows and fret marks, your flesh clear of contortions and contusions—what could such a death possibly bespeak but a life of meticulous disengagement?

Unless, of course, you are very, very young.

*

LXIII

In this realm where happiness is contagious, you can determine the level of a citizen's emotional maturity by observing whether that individual chooses to approach or to avoid the unremittingly cheerful, who, sad to say, comprise an ever-greater proportion of the populace.

*

LXIV

This realm existed for only the single hour during which its three inhabitants sustained it by their conviction that because of the sudden luminous hyperclarity of their immediate environment (which happened to be an alehouse), they were already residing in the afterlife.

Their belief was completely unfalsifiable; if one of them had happened to drop dead within that time, the others would have assumed that their comrade had been sent back to the land of mortals to assist those still waiting to cross over.

*

LXV

This is the realm upon which everything depends. Here in a lead safe cemented deep beneath the fountain in The Beautiful Plaza waits the "reserve story" that will sustain the universe when all the combinations of plots throughout all of the realms have at last been depleted.

A few people whisper that this is a myth promulgated by the powers-that-be in order to stave off the threat of social chaos—there is no safe under the fountain, just dirt and rocks. According to a related rumor, there is indeed a safe, but it is empty—while some assert that this is the same as there being no safe at all, others maintain that a vacant safe not only constitutes a story in and of itself, but serves by definition as the only story that could never be "used up."

Almost everyone, however, believes fervently in the reserve story. In fact, the only reason people from other realms don't make pilgrimages to the site is that this realm is far too small to accommodate such devotions. It consists of nothing but the Plaza, a pleasant cobblestone span swept once a week or so by volunteers from a neighboring realm who tote their own brooms and dustpans across the border.

*

Claire Bateman's books are: *The Bicycle Slow Race* (Wesleyan University Press, 1991), *Friction* (Eighth Mountain Poetry Prize, 1998), *At the Funeral of the Ether* (Ninety-Six Press, 1998), *Clumsy* (New Issues Poetry & Prose, 2003), *Leap* (New Issues, 2005), *Coronology* (a chapbook, single long poem, Serving House Books, 2009), *Coronology* (and other poems) (Etruscan Press, 2010), and *Locals* (Serving House Books, 2012). She has been awarded Individual Artist Fellowships from the National Endowment for the Arts, the Tennessee Arts Commission, and the Surdna Foundation, as well as two Pushcart Prizes. She has taught at Clemson University, the Fine Arts Center of Greenville, SC, and various workshops and conferences. She lives in Greenville, SC, and is poetry editor of the *St. Katherine Review*.

www.ingramcontent.com/pod-product-compliance
Lightning Source LLC
Chambersburg PA
CBHW051849040426
42447CB00006B/762